Angles

Kristen OGorman

BookLeaf Publishing

India | USA | UK

Presentation by *BookLeaf Publishing*

Web: www.bookleafpub.com

E-mail: info@bookleafpub.com

ISBN: 9789358314298

First edition 2024

DEDICATION

To those closest to me,

May this book inspire your imagination and fuel your dreams. I dedicate these words to you and the boundless possibilities that await you.

ACKNOWLEDGEMENT

I want to thank everyone and everything for providing inspiration, whether sad, happy, angry, beautiful, or ugly.

PREFACE

I have considered the many inclinations and perceptions of my life a great deal—all the time. I honestly never stop, but I used to write all the time. I used to adore it. Then, one day, I quit. I didn't look back. I didn't want to for a vast number of reasons. Putting myself and my thoughts out there for the world to terrorize is not easy for me. Opening up about much of anything is challenging for me. So, this body of writing is me not only beginning to write again, to feel passionate about something, well, anything again, and to force myself to get out from under my anxieties about sharing out loud and taking up space. It's also about giving you my slant thoughts to see from your angles, and I hope you do.

Privation

I still miss you
like a body part,
ripped from inside me.
My shattered spirit, slowly glued,
piece by piece,
back together,
missing its animated light.
Passion, a wildfire,
burned me to ash.
A heart dimmed.
Healing slow,
it is hard to express,
define,
to keep within boundaries.
The feeling of loss,
heavy,
tingling,
like a phantom limb.
I'll miss you
for the rest of my time.

Ghostly limbs are tricky,
and,
coupled with a mind
of betrayal,

cause considerable,
mental warfare.
So, I learn to live with,
and without.
A boundaryless realm
of gray and blue,
of depravities hue.
Until,
One day, red,
reintroduced,
reminds me
that blood still fills
my internal webbing.
Pumping.
Beating.
Pulsating.
Spirit smolders,
sparks,
and bursts into light.
Passion begins anew.

Ocean

It would be easy for me to let go,
to drift with the wild tide,
into dancing, spiritual winds,
inside the unhinged current
of a monochromatic blue void.
I feel eternally calm as
the impartial waves batter me.
I flip forward,
sideways,
backward.
The soft skin of my back
scrapes the coarse ocean floor,
a gentle sensation at first.
My feet, unsteady,
pull and sink,
pull and sink.
Eccentric, salt-drenched waves
bulldoze me to an indifferent shore
while the grainy sands beneath
drag lifeless ankles outward.
I fumble clumsily,
pulling,
pulling,
until- Yes!
At long last,

my loose footing catches
and willfully
digs calloused heels in.
I Stand.
Exfoliated.
Breathless.
Choking.
Salty water slowly drips,
drips,
drips,
from all orifices,
burning my yellow-ringed blue eyes.
The skin of my sensitive back
loudly prickling.
I think, "I could be liberated,
just...
float away into oblivion.".
Yet, I feel vitality in my veins.
Exhilarating.
Thriving.
Pulsating.
My humming nervous system
propels me.
Sun, salt, and sand-drenched hairs
plaster against my forehead,
cling to my neck.
I Pause.
Catch my renewed breath.
One.

Two.
Three.
RUN.
Run fast.
Run hard.
Animated Body
and vibrant mind
begging
and
pleading
for more,
for something greater,
and more significant than myself.

You Have Told Lies

You have told lies, and you have told the truth,
but I just could not tell the difference.
I said you don't care; you have little proof.

Picture me, disguised as abhorrent sleuths,
organizing fibs without preference.
You have told lies, and you have told the truth.

There was little to be said that would soothe.
Each slight, by design, had consequences.
I said you don't care; you have little proof.

Each snake lash of your tongue did not behoove.
Yet, fires of hope burned in defiance.
You have told lies, and you have told the truth.

I fell, a sad creature broke and uncouth,
knelt before you, devoid of inference.
I said you don't care; you have little proof.

You sat, head in your hands, trying to soothe,
Refrained, explained, begged for deliverance.
You have told lies, and you have told the truth.
I said you don't care; you have little proof.

Crisp Senses

Autumn,
Smells spiced and sweet,
Tastes rich and of the earth.
Fires breathe comfort, sparking warm,
Whispers.

Spin Doctor

Deceiving all honor,
disrupting truth's blurred line of light.
I feel your pain; I do.
No cure inside the guts of life,
the spirit's anger strikes.
The raindrops beat my mind to sleep,
exhausted by your drive.
You're even scheming time, my friend.

Existence warped by all your talk,
lie after lie, you tell,
until false becomes truth; it's fused.
You light it up and smile
to watch unhinged, to feel content.
The shaky ethics hurt,
but not to you. How does that feel?
You CONvince them you're more,
afraid they'll see to it you aren't.

Exploitation

I'm not about to live out life
as a composting bin
for bosses hurling out their strife,
a stepping stone to win.

I'm not manure creator -rife
nutrients for your win-
a garden growing, change of life -
for you - me left therein!

Queen Life

She can be generous in her endeavors;
be terrible to her subjects - horrific!
She thrives everywhere/nowhere whatsoever.
Her name's, tripped from unsettled lips, prolific.

Heartbeats and breathing aren't anything
without.
She offers, she offers sans shadows of doubt.
It was her love that started the world we know.
Her love will end souls, a spectacle or so.

Countercurrent

A dark vortex
Inside me
Mind twists
Fraught
Frayed
Faster than
The spinning
World
Hunched shoulders
Anxiety

Neglect

A boy - ruffled hair and baggy clothes
From somewhere in the trailer park
Sat on a railroad tie - sad
He pulls, tugs, and tears at
Stretching blades of grass
Hunching Shoulders
Disturbed eyes
Alone
Hurt

Aftershocks

I was Vesuvius and Pompeii,
A raging storm slamming everything around
you.
What could a healing person say?

Water swirled in our eyes with love,
but they,
filled with hurt, humiliation, anger, and
deception too.
I was Vesuvius and Pompeii.

You spilled too late apologies, like milk, after I
lost my way.
There's no sense in crying over that, too; it's
true.
What could a healing person say?

I don't deal in what-ifs, and you deserved the
bed you made
Long after we began healing, you spilled your
heart - I withdrew.
I was Vesuvius and Pompeii.

Your heart, a mighty river, ran through my
fingers - ran away.

I tried, tried, tried to build a dam- to hold it
back- so I didn't lose it, I didn't lose you.
What could a healing person say?

But you see, I don't deal in what-ifs or shades of
gray
All our once whole particles became shattered
soldiers - withdrew!
I was Vesuvius and Pompeii.
What could a healing person say?

Callous

I have starved myself to learn lessons.
I've fed myself well to compare.
My mind has warred with depression.
I have shattered into infinite air.
I've changed faces for first impressions.
Set my soul on fire, skin bared.

But who am I now? Do I care?

Your eyes held the light - a thousand candles!
Eyes burned holes through limitless darkness,
a sad void of gold-woven brambles,
that once flickered to life with such sharpness.
My favorite moment, yet least treasured scandal,
Because your soul boasts an ironic starkness.

But where are you now? Are you, too, heartless?

Sunburn

Some parts of life are so far
out of my hands.
It hurts even to consider them.
The cloud of my rain once deserted me.
The sun to my moon soon followed.
It was brilliant once.
Wasn't it?
You, dear sun,
begged me to live,
And once I did,
hanging,
upside down -
from the top bar,
of a swing set.
You kissed me,
and,
together we radiated.
I felt your light,
but could no longer,
trust its warmth.
How long would it last,
ever threaded,
and weaving,
with the moon,
through darkness?

And dear sun,
you burned a hole,
in my chest -
left a pang,
of regret,
in my stomach.
I cooled until I froze;
Then I shred myself,
shed my skin,
so you could start fresh,
so you could sparkle,
without guilt again.

Introverts

People like me,
Make people like you,
Uncomfortable,
Silence-loving people,
Like me
Make noise-filling-rooms-people,
Like you,
Feel awkward.
We're too weird for you,
Too socially broken, and,
Stigmatized to be wrong.
Your vampiric nature,
Hates us,
And,
Our Boundaries.
Your soul-sucking energies,
Feed off our humiliations.
Because we can't, socially,
Feed your fragile egos.

People like me,
We'd try to show you,
That we're different,
From what you think,
But you'd never hear,

US,
Over the sound,
Of your voice,
Anyway,
You're incapable,
UNLESS,
We expend the energy,
To yell over you.
We never will.
Why would we?
We need that energy,
To keep us socially warm,
Because society is,
UNWHOLE,
BROKEN,
UNJUST,
CRUEL,
LOUD,
EXTROVERTED,
UNSYMPATHETIC,
And achingly COLD.
So, we just stare.
Blankly.
Blinking.
Blinking,
To hold back,
Our internal screams,
While our immune systems,
Consume our bodies,

OUR BODIES.
People like me.

Depression

21

Depression is an oil slick.
I slid in, darkness and grease all over me,
and slipped into hell with its tricks.
Depression is an oil slick.
My mind screams, fights, and kicks.
My body is gloom's, numb, devotee.
Depression is an oil slick -
a black-stained nervous system in a hoodie

Simple Evening

Sitting up, leaning to the right side,
beneath a gray, fuzzy blanket,
in PJs and a hoodie,
bold black lettering scrawled -
"Je T'aime A' Mourir".
You're beside me.
I feel warm.
Happy.
Full.

No Room

23

Lately, you've felt there's no room for you
anywhere,
Like a chair that won't fit at a table -
An out-of-place object, making them stare.
Lately, you've felt there's no room for you
anywhere,
Feeling lonely, awkward, and scared.
Someone might say, "This piece isn't right. It's a
little unstable."
Lately, you've felt there is no room for you
anywhere,
Like a chair that won't fit at a table.

What you are

You're not as bad as -
or - what people think you are.
Also, to point out,
you're not your own thoughts of self.
You are electricity.

Seeing through

25

I've never trusted the windows!
Others see light shine through,
I spy a weakness for dark goals-
crashing, cracking, in two.

The threats of all of the weirdos,
lingers above the few!
They drill out our mind's blackest holes.
Would you trust if you knew?

Growing older

Green eyes - which can sometimes appear gray-
once sprinkled with laughter and joy,
now lay claim to the consequential nature of
fate.
Her smile, once beaming and bright, was now
coy
from years of suffering life's unrelenting noise.
Strength's grown tall in those no longer gullible
delicate features.
Sadness, now a permanent mask, lays upon her
brow to exploit
the light and airy way she once moved through a
crowd of nonbelievers.
For SHE is the high priestess of the most
melancholic creatures.

A Cycle of Faith

Head in my hands, feeling used and alone,
Heart of crumbs, and everyone is lying,
No one cares for trust, like money - like groans!
Is it collected and saved for dying?

After death, then how is trust spent - on fate?
What's faith but a chameleon that blends blight,
Losing its tail, growing it back - a wraith.
Creed is playing with darkness to gain light.

You stole trust and faith, double-dealing lies.
People told me I was fine - not my mind!
Glowing embers fight in lines as allies.
Ideals do not convince me; I'm hope blind.

But a flower throws scent beneath a shoe
And a longing love in me breathed and grew.

Suicidal Ideation

Being here is like living in a permanent sentence
fragment.
What you thought you knew or heard ends
abruptly before your mind.
Is this the absolute best you've got, the best you
can be?
Sometimes, you disappear but then must return
stagnant.
You communicate without sound, without
wonder.
Feeling stuck and cold inside, You want to run.
Are you but an outcast within the sun?
A minute soul creating thunder?
You try hard to cut yourself loose,
to feel the warm beam instead.
You want this skin to shed,
heart to lack abuse.
"Picture a gun
to my head",
You said.
Stunned.

www.ingramcontent.com/pod-product-compliance
Lightning Source LLC
LaVergne TN
LVHW010948200726
843509LV00013B/2318